Lord, I Want To CELEBRATE

Lord, I Want To CELEBRATE

Prayer Exercises by
Richard W. Bimler
and
Prayers by
Herbert F. Brokering

CONCORDIA®

Publishing House
St. Louis

Photos by Wallowitch

Concordia Publishing House, St. Louis, Missouri

Manufactured in the United States of America

CONTENTS

This life-centered book combines 99 prayers with realistic experiences to create a spirit of celebration. *Lord, I Want to Celebrate* is written for youth and for persons young in spirit. Each prayer by Herbert Brokering and accompanying prayer exercise by Richard Bimler deals with one vital aspect of life. It directs the thoughts and feelings of youth to the festivity they have in Jesus Christ. The love and forgiveness of Christ and the many gifts of the Holy Spirit are viewed in a variety of ways. These prayers and spiritual events point to Christian joy and celebration.

Thus the title of the book, *Lord, I Want to Celebrate.*

The poem-prayers and exercises have these main concerns: Self-Concept; Gratitude; Emotions; Relationship to God; Nature; Resurrection and Sacrament; and Changes.

Use the book for personal and group devotion; in public worship; in small groups, class, and family devotions; for youth gatherings and retreats; during confirmation; with friends; and as families.

Each page can become a large event or discussion. Or the book may provide for a personal and private reflection in spirituality. It can be used loudly, or quietly.

Lord, I Want to Celebrate lends itself to a variety of uses—read portions aloud, put some lines to music, read it responsively in worship, develop or extend favorite ideas, study it in the classroom, create a prayer program series, share parts with friends and family.

Choose any part of the book, and you have a prayer meeting. Any page can offer an enriching quiet time. Any section can stir up a discussion for a day, or a weekend.

This book is a perfect gift for confirmands. It can lead youth and leaders in their daily prayer life. Youth counselors will find the book a stimulating guide into the congregation's life, prayer, and mission.

Lord, I Want to Celebrate is a new type of book for a very old human need—prayer life.

Richard Bimler and Herbert Brokering are known in the world of youth and worship for their Biblical, creative, and spirit-filled imaginations. In this book, the authors bring their many years of youth leadership, sensitivity, and theology directly to youth. It is a personal tribute to youth in faith.

This book seems to answer an old church question: What does life mean to me? The psalmist asked, the reformers asked, and we ask. The answer still leads to confession and to celebration.

Lord, I Want to Celebrate is a new kind of book.

SELF-CONCEPT

CELEBRATION

Lord, I want to celebrate
what I see and what I ate,
what it means to run or wait,
become fifty or turn eight.
Lord, I want to celebrate
when a story is turned straight,
when forgiving is not late,
when a wall becomes a gate.
Lord, I want to celebrate,
what is small and what is great.
Help my spirit integrate
all the life You generate.

This book is about celebration! Enjoy these pages as you celebrate inside the Lord's presence.

Read these prayers one at a time, skip around the book, choose your favorites. Use it the way it fits best in your schedule.

Put these prayers to music, select your favorites and send them to a friend, write your own. And continue to look to God as the source of your celebrations.

LORD OF ME

Lord of life, and Lord of me,
thanks for making me to see,
that Your love is constantly
shaping worlds inside of me.

Write a special prayer and thank God for making you.

Plan to use a special gift for someone else today.

Shout hooray three times (or more) and share the joy of the Lord with someone each day. For the Lord of life is the Lord of us all!

GENERATIONS

Lord of each new generation,
send to us Your inspiration
that in our imagination
we will know regeneration.
> Meet us in our meditation
> by a birth of inspiration
> in our daily celebration.
Lord, unfold this generation
with Your holy inspiration,
so we have rejuvenation
through a quiet contemplation.

This prayer talks about the different generations. The Lord is Lord of all of them. Take time this week to talk to people younger and older than you—grandmas, little five year olds; middle-aged people. Just share a little bit about yourself, your faith, your life. And ask them to do the same.

Ask a senior citizen and an elementary-aged youngster to read this prayer and explain what it means to them. Share your own feelings with them.

As the last line suggests, take time out today to be by yourself and quietly contemplate your life and faith in the Lord. Plan to spend time alone each day for this sharing.

MARRIAGE

Lord,
I saw the flower bloom
then the fragrance filled the room;
one was bride and one was groom.
I was watching in this room.
Lord,
I saw the ring in hand,
chosen ring, a wedding band.
Goldest ring in all the land.
I was looking at the hand.
Lord,
Keep me alive to what is true,
what is old and what is new.
With the many, with the few
keep affection in my view.
Keep commitment in my view.

Ask someone married what marriage vows are. Get a number of opinions on it.

What kind of partner would you want if you chose to get married? What would be important for you in a marriage partner?

Ask someone married to recall for you their wedding day—what remembrances of it do they have? Ask them questions about it.

ARGUMENTS

Lord,
the arguments get very loud;
we are lost inside some cloud,
feelings tight in twisted shroud,
hasty words are garbles loud.
Why this arguing so loud?

Lord ot humble, God of proud,
lift my thoughts on top a cloud,
fly, and break this twisted shroud.

Think of how you feel when there is an argument in your family. Whose fault are they? Who usually wins? Who starts them? How do you feel about all of this?

Think of how you react to arguments in your home. Do you ignore them? Become a big part of them? Do they really bother you?

Ask God to continue to help you love and share your feelings during family troubles. Pray that you do not overreact or take sides. Pray that you can be a person who forgives and helps others to love and forgive too.

AGES

Lord, I was two and I was five,
Both in me are quite alive.
I was five and I was nine,
These two ages both were Thine.
I was one and I was three.
Both of these are inside me.
Lord of ages, God of time,
keep alive all years of mine.

What was your favorite age? Why? Ask others about their favorite age.

What age would you like to be right now? Why? Check out this with others, too.

Think of significant happenings to you during the last five years. What would you like to have happen in the next five years?

FENCES

Lord, I'm tired of this fence,
never knowing where or whence
of my simple circumstance.
I keep falling off my fence.
Lord, give to me more confidence.
Give to me more evidence
so I will not fear this fence,
so I grow in confidence.

Identify a fence in your life. What makes you unsure of yourself and keeps you from growing?

Identify fences that other people have. How can you help someone to work through a problem?

Forgiveness comes through Christ's death and resurrection for us. He frees us from our fences and says, "You are forgiven!" Enjoy that gift today!

SEXUALITY

Lord, inside the Trinity,
forming life and energy
save me from monotony.
Send the gift of mystery
and the sense of-charity
to my sexuality.
Save me in the mystery
of all force and energy.

What is sexuality? Ask some of your friends and family and see what different definitions you hear.

Check out some radio, TV, and newspaper ads this week. What do they seem to be saying about sex and sexuality?

God created people as sexual beings. Sex is a gift from God. Enjoy your sexuality! Marvel at the mystery of it all. See it as a gift from God.

Sexuality is intricately related to the whole person. Do you see this relationship?

DEATH

Lord,
I do not wish to die,
leave this earth of sea and sky,
stop the fun of asking why,
feel the leap of low and high.
Lord, it sometimes makes me cry
just to think that I will die.
Can you tell me why, oh, why
when Your Son was soon to die,
He did kneel and almost cry?
Ask you if and ask you why?
So you surely must know why,
why I sometimes wonder why.

Are you afraid to die? It is helpful to talk about your feelings and thoughts with someone close to you. Seek out someone this week.

Why do you think some people are afraid to die?

Is it wrong to be afraid to die? Why?

Who do you know facing death?

QUESTIONING

Lord,
how does evening turn to night?
Why do some grown people fight?
Where does meekness store its might?
How does midnight become light?
What makes Easter time so bright?
How does hatred turn contrite?
When do blind still have their sight?
Lord of miracles and night,
give my eyes a second sight.

The struggle between being a sinner and a saint at the same time is in all of us. Recall today when your "sinner" came through louder than your "saint." What can you do about it?

The brightness of Easter makes us saints—Christ's death and resurrection make it possible for our sinful life to be a saint-ful life. Thank the Lord for Easter in some special way—blow up a balloon, make a poster, shout hooray, kiss a baby, share your faith with someone.

Make a special prayer list for people who are experiencing some pain and despair. Pray for them regularly.

TOUCH

Lord of distance, God of touch,
reach us when we have too much.
Span the distance to each star.
Take us where the angels are
so our mind will travel far
where the holy regions are.
Lord of little, God of much,
meet us in each tiny touch;
be the God of those and such
living in your magic touch.

God touches us in many ways. How has God touched you today? Share.

Physical touch is an important gift. After sharing this prayer, choose a few people to touch in some way—a hug, a kiss, a handshake, a good word. Do it. They will be "touched" too.

God touches us with love in many ways. Keep this touch through a regular sharing of the Scriptures. Read the Gospel of John, for a refresher, and see how this Gospel is touching.

SIGHT AND SOUND

Lord, my hearing, God, my eyes
    need the joy of quick surprise,
    need the wonder of the why's,
    need to hear the nation's cries.
Give us wisdom, make us wise.
    Send the joy of quick surprise
    as a Holy Spirit prize
    to our inner spirit eyes.

Spend a few minutes just listening—to anything around you. Identify the different sounds.

Do the same by just looking around you and taking in all the sights your eyes can see. Try to find little things that you often fail to see in your daily life.

Thank the Lord for the gifts of sight and sound today. And use these gifts to enjoy and relate God's goodness.

TRAVELERS

Lord of travelers on the go,
watch us as we come and go,
see the swallows flying low,
    send the wind to whisk and blow,
hear the earthworms down below,
    watch the mountain flowers grow,
frozen rocks that heave and ho,
    angel choirs, chanting so,
fishermen who row and row,
Lord of travelers on the go
show us what we ought to know.

Say a special prayer for any travelers today. Pray that they reach their destination.

Use this prayer on your next trip. Think of other prayers for travelers while you're traveling. Have everyone who is traveling with you develop some prayers, also.

Where would you like to travel? Why? Consider ways to make a trip come true!

SERVANTHOOD

> Lord,
> I see the Babel tower
> skyscrapers that would devour
> little stores and tiny shop.
> Cement is reaping bumper crop.
> Lord, I feel the Babel tower
> climbing higher by the hour,
> some possessed with building power.
> Help me know when I must stop
> in this building up and up.
> Lord, why was it You came down
> to a small Judean town?

When do you find yourself trying to build yourself up to someone? What do you say to others in order to make a good impression on them?

Jesus came to be a servant to all of us. He asks that we too become servants to the people around us. Think of some way to serve someone special today.

Have you ever done something for someone that you really didn't want to do? What was it? Why did you do it? Read John 13, and share the contents with a friend.

Do you know persons who are servant-like? Talk to them. How does one become such a minister?

SELF-REFLECTION

Lord, the people look at me.
What on earth is there to see
that they all do stare at me?
Lord, the people ask me "why,"
when I'm quiet, when I sigh,
act as though I must not cry.
Lord of all who come and go,
look me over head to toe,
till I know You love me so.

What do people think of you? How would your best friends describe you? Would you agree? Why or why not?

Write down some good characteristics you have. Think of good things to say about yourself. Fill a page or two. Don't be modest; do be honest. How does this make you feel?

Ask some good friends and family to do the same thing for themselves and also for you. You write down their best characteristics, too. Then compare the results.

Be thankful that the Lord sees all of us as redeemed people. God looks at us through the cross and empty tomb and sees saved and celebrative people. God says, "You are My own." And I'm glad!

YES AND NO

Lord, I'm full of "Don't" and "No."
People shout, "I told you so!"
Where do loving "Yesses" go?
Why do wheels of cannons go
where the purple violets grow?
Search me, Lord, from head to toe;
give me back the inner glow
so I know You love is so.

Make a list of how many "yes" and "no" thoughts you heard today; that is, how many times people affirmed others and criticized others.

Who are "yes" people in your life?

Who are "no" people in your life? Are some people on both lists?

Are you a "yes" person or a "no" person? Think about what you say and feel about certain other people.

Thank God for all the "yes" statements in your life. And thank God for both the "yes" people and the "no" people in your life. Jesus is God's YES. Share this with those around you!

Look at 2 Corinthians 1:19-24. Celebrate today that Christ is God's YES to you!

GOALS

Lord,
I think I've lost my goal,
lost direction of my soul.
Make me one till I am whole.
    Lord, I fell inside a hole,
    couldn't see a single soul,
    lost my name and lost my role.
Lord, I think I see my goal,
since Your Spirit has control.
Join the pieces of my soul
till they make one holy whole.

List out for yourself three to five goals you have for your life.

Share these goals with someone close to you. Listen to the reactions and comments.

Now list some barriers that have gotten in your way of reaching your goals. Share these with someone else, and consider ways of overcoming these barriers.

WORDS THAT SEPARATE

Lord,
hear the words that separate:
"Watch your step" and "Stand up straight."
"Where were you," "It is so late!"
"You be quiet," "Let's relate."
"Close the door;" and "Shut the gate."
"Don't you ever dare be late."
　　　Lord, you know how much I hate
　　　all the words that separate.
　　　Lord, I want to celebrate
　　　even when I'm wrong or late.

Are these some of the words you hear at school or home or church? Recall the context in which they were spoken.

Words can separate people from each other. They can also bring people closer together. Make a list of words that separate, and a list of words that draw people together. Which words do you hear more often? Which do you hear least often?

God gives us the joy and power of forgiveness to share with those who wrong us. Why not try to share that forgiveness with someone close to you today?

GRATITUDE

GIFTS AND GIVING

Lord,
I have something nice today
that I'd like to give away.
It's a very simple thing;
it's my midweek offering.
Could it be a thing to sing?
Could it join a bird on wing?
Could it be a golden ring?
Could it be a thoughtful thing?
Lord,
I have something nice to give;
it may help another live.
If I give this gift away
help me give the gift today.

What could you give to someone close to you that would be very helpful and important to this person? Why not do it today?

What would you like to receive from someone today? How will you react if it happens? If it doesn't happen?

List things you could give to four or five of your special people. Work on giving them this during this month. Thank the Lord for daily gifts—and for special people.

THANKS!

Lord, the price is high to pay
if You charge me for this day.
> Lord, what would You ask of me
> if this day I paid a fee?
Lord, the price is high to pay
if You charged for all You say.
> Lord, what would You ask of me
> if this new day were not free?
Lord, the price is very high to pay.
"Thanks," is all I wish to pray.

What kind of day did you have today? Reflect on what made it that kind of day.

God gives us each a new day as a free gift, to enjoy, to use, to celebrate. How did you use this gift today? Think of ways you could have used it differently.

God cares about the way we use each day. Look ahead to tomorrow and ask the Lord for a special measure of His presence, in order to use the day in the best way you can. And it's all free for the asking!

RHYTHM AND RHYME

Lord of rhythm, Lord of rhyme,
join me to Your tidal time.
Lord of millions, Lord of dime,
bless big books and bless this rhyme.

God is the Lord of all of life. Say a special prayer to God today.

What does this prayer say to you? Discuss it with someone special.

We have a Lord of little things and big things. Imagine five good big things the Lord has given you. When you have reflected on them, tell them to someone who will be glad to listen.

SURPRISE!

Lord,
how good that we can be amazed,
that You are such a Friend and yet You can be praised.
So with the angels we can, too, be dazed,
and You can warm our faith when hope is cold and glazed.
Lord, each day I wish my spirit to be re-amazed.
And, in amazement, You by me be praised,
and praised and praised and praised.

Think of a surprise that has happened to you recently. Thank the Lord for all the surprises in your life.

Take a look at the hymn, "What a Friend We Have in Jesus." Read the words to yourself—and even sing the verses if you wish. Thank the Lord for being your Friend—and also your Redeemer! Can you think of other "friendly" songs?

Look around you and make a list of five things that amaze you about your Lord. Do it for the next couple of days and see what kind of list you can create.

THANKSGIVING

Lord of tree and forest fire,
lightning rod and 'lectric wire,
bubbling spring and ocean wave,
come and see and come to save.
Lord of snow and winter wheat,
give us milk and bread to eat.
Lord of silver, gold, and dust,
teach us how to thank and trust.

Thanksgiving is every day. Make a list of what you are thankful for today.

Share this prayer with some friends or a group of people. Write one of your own about some of the gifts of God.

Start a file of words and pictures that remind you of things for which you are thankful. Make a collage with them for your wall.

OFFERINGS

Lord, thank You for the harvest moon,
the mockingbird, the diving loon,
the ocean tide and sandy dune.
All these are in my offering plate,
all these and more reconsecrate.
Lord, thank You for the Easter moon,
for surprise when snow comes soon,
for highest sun in summer noon.
All these are in my offering.
All these and more to You I bring.

God gives us gifts to use and share with others. List some special gifts you have.

How do you use these gifts? Think of other ways to use your gifts for the people around you.

Our whole life becomes our offering to God. It's not what we put into the offering plates on Sunday morning; instead, we offer our lives to the Lord through sharing our lives with others. Make it a point to especially use some of your gifts today for those around you.

BIG AND SMALL

Lord of all the girls and boys,
teddy bears and plastic toys,
keep unfolding joy on joys.
Lord of all the big and small,
when I stumble, when I fall
make my spirit strong and tall.
Lord of all the brown and white,
yellow bird and torn kite,
give me wings for my next flight.

Read this prayer with a young brother or sister or friend.
Ask them what it means.

Write a poem or draw a picture that shares the fact that
the Lord protects and loves all people. Show it to someone.

The Lord is Lord of all things! Shout a big hooray! If
someone asks why, tell them.

POTTER AND CLAY

Lord,
if in the closing of this day
nothing seems for sure to stay,
be the Potter, I the clay.
I the clay go whirling round,
of this spirit of the ground,
I am shaped and I am found
in this spinning round and round.

Recall your birth. Ask your parents for some of the details
of this big event.

We are created by God as special people. We are shaped by God's love and forgiveness. Talk to a little child today about how important she is in God's sight.

What kind of day did you have today? A good one, or a bad one? Regardless of what happened, end your day today by thanking God for making you. You are special! Rejoice in that! And have a good day tomorrow—in the name of the Lord!

LORD OF ALL

Lord of south and God of west,
join the bird in summer nest.
Join the deer as winter guest.
Join the traveler in the rest.
Join the children in their test.
Join the minstrel inside zest.

Lord of east and God of west,
join us in the worst and best.

The Lord watches over His creation and is active in the story of life. What is a meaning this prayer has for you?

Think of specific people or places where you would expect God to be at this very moment. Say a prayer for these special people and places. And rest assured that He is there.

Sometimes we feel that God is not with us. Have you ever felt this way? When? Share your feelings with a friend. Discuss ways to help each other know that God is always present.

PEACE

Lord of highs and God of lows,
keep me on my feet and toes;
fill me up when power goes.
Bless the wind the autumn blows.
Send the peace Your Spirit knows.

Say a quiet hooray to yourself or someone. God is alive and living with you! Share that joy with someone else!

Select words that share how you feel about the Lord. Hang them up in your room as a "faith lift" for you. Add other words that come to mind.

Use this prayer whenever you feel down and depressed. It reminds us that God is Lord of all and continues to send peace.

EMOTIONS

TEARS AND FEARS

Lord, I drown inside my fears.
Lord, my eyes are full of tears.
Can I live inside my fears?
Oh, the sound of taunting jeers
of some elders and some peers.
Whisper through my tears and fears
till I hear You in my ears.

Sometimes it seems that everyone is against us. Has this ever happened to you? What do you do about it?

What difference does it make to know that the Lord is with you, even when it seems that most everyone else is turning on you?

This week see if you can find someone who feels that the world is falling down. Try sharing a kind word and deed with this person.

LONELY

Lord, I feel this silent wall,
thick as fog, so deep and tall.
Keep me safe from any fall.
Hear my sudden frightened call

when temptation makes me fall.
Lord of stars and manger stall,
be the Lord and God of all.

Most people have felt lonely and alone many times in their lives. They feel they are caught in a fog, a silent wall. What do you do when you feel alone?

Draw a picture of how it looks when you feel alone.   33

Discuss this picture with someone else. What are some meanings you find in it? Share them.

Finish this sentence: "A silent wall in my life is . . ."

NIGHT

Lord,
lead me through the fears of night.
Break the grip of darkest fright
that would dim my sound and sight.
If some fear I need to fight
give me strength and give me light.
Keep me safe as birds in flight.
Help me, please, all through the night.

Night time can be a time for fear and loneliness. How do you feel about the night? What are favorite things you do at night?

It is good to know that our Lord is always with us—day and night. What are some ways you remember that fact? How do you use symbols, pictures, drawings, jewelry, or souvenirs to remember that God is your comfort and that God is present with you?

ANGER

Lord, stand back and see my temper fly.
I holler, "Me?" I holler, "Why?"
My holler rises to Your sky.
My whisper turns into a cry;
my anger turns into a lie.
So many things I want to do.
Sometimes the choices seem too few.
I'm telling all of this to You
to make my spirit become new.
Guide me daily through this day,
lest some hate lead me astray.

Think of things that make you angry. Make a list of them.

Why do these things upset you?

What can you do about it? Try talking to a friend about them. Share some of your feelings with someone you feel close to—or someone who you think will listen to you. Go ahead! Give it a try.

HIGHS AND LOWS

Lord of valleys, God of sky,
when my spirit seems too high
stars keep falling from my sky.
Sometimes all I ask is "Why?"
Love and beauty pass me by.
God of feelings low and high
while I worry, while I cry,
send Your Spirit to my sky.

How does this poem make you feel? Have you ever had a day like that? Try to recall.

How can you help someone who is having such a day? What would you say? What would you do? Rehearse it. What would you want to have someone else say to you if you were that person?

Look in the Bible and pick out places that remind you that our Lord is always loving and caring for us. One place to start is Matthew 8.

What stories did you hear as a child that are like this prayer?

RENEWAL

Lord of future and newborn,
You know love can get too worn.
A lengthy friendship can get torn,
and old love can be reborn.
You know the feelings of forlorn
can be like new by early morn.
Lord of tatters, God of torn,
span my life from dusk to morn
so I, too, may be reborn,
in a world so hurt and torn.

Think of two or three people who are hurting today because of something that has happened to them. Say a prayer for them.

When is the last time you were disappointed in someone else? Recall the situation and reflect on your feelings.

And now rejoice that God forgives and sets us right again, even in the midst of a world that gives us grief and pain.

MOODS

Lord,
You know me by the way I brood,
the way I worry, by my mood.
I'm torn between the things I should,
and then between the things I would,
and sometimes by the things I could.
I thank You, Lord, for You are good
to keep in mind my daily mood
and help me feel I'm understood.

During this week, make a list of how you feel each day. Graph it out, according to a "high" day, and a "low" day.

What does it say to you today? That you know that God loves you—just the way you are?

How can you share this love with others, and with yourself?

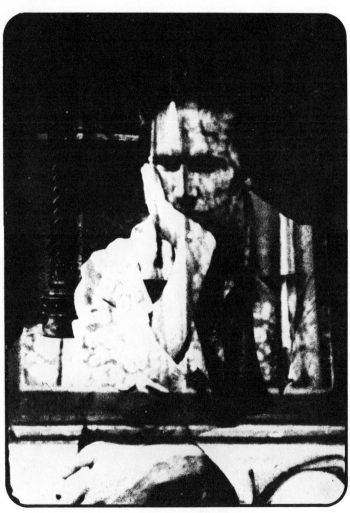

FEELINGS

Lord, You can hear and You can heal,
all the weeping I conceal.
Quiet me, so I can kneel.
Meet me in Your holy meal
where in mercy You will heal.

Feelings are real. Feelings can get us down or make us high. List how you feel today: I FEEL . . .

Now ask yourself why you feel this way today. What has happened to make you feel this way? Identify where your feelings come from.

Share these prayer thoughts with a friend of yours. Discuss together what the words mean to you. How does the Lord's Supper fit into these thoughts.

INSIDE FEELINGS

Lord,
there are feelings inside me
none can tell or ever see,
sad and glad as they can be.
Lord,
there are feelings on my mind,
thoughts and words of every kind,
hard to hide and hard to find.
Lord,
there are feelings on my tongue,
high and low as ever sung,
free as bird and feelings flung.
Lord,
there are feelings in my heart,
some at peace and some apart.
Make me sure how great Thou art.

How are you feeling right now? Think of a word or two that describes your feeling. Why are you feeling this way?

Which six words describe how you usually feel? What makes you change feelings every day or week or hour?

The Lord accepts our questions and helps us to know that God loves us always. Feelings are not good or bad—they are real—they are you. Rejoice in the Lord by shouting, "How Great Thou Art!"

LIGHTS

Lord,
the arrows point both left and right,
arrows flashing in the night,
blinking red and yellow light.
What a gawdy, awesome sight,
flashing comfort, flashing fright
up and down, to left and right,
arrows flashing out of sight.
Lord, You asked that there be light.
Neon, sun, and candlelight.

List as many highway signals as you can think of. What do most signals try to say to the driver?

The next time you see a red light or a blinking light or a turn signal, be reminded of the Lord who is the Light of the World. Let this be a good visual aid to help you see the presence of the Lord.

What signals frighten you? Which ones are comforting to you? What kind of signal do you send to people you meet or who see you, in terms of your faith in the Lord of Light? Discuss and share.

UPS AND DOWNS

Lord,
there is this going up and down
in my home and in my town,
every person like a clown
making laughter, forming frown.
Love goes up and then goes down
in my home and in my town.
Lord of going round and round
mix Your word in wind and sound.
Life will leap and love abound
in between the sky and ground.
Lord of countryside and town,
make of me a holy clown
in this going up and down.

What kind of day did you have today? An "up" or "down" day? Why was it so? How would you draw or sketch this day?

Some people call Christians "fools for Christ," or clowns. Do you ever picture yourself as a fool, or clown, for Christ? When?

Even though our lives may go up and down depending on what is happening in our daily experiences, the Lord's love for us is always "up." That is, it's always constant. Share this fact with someone who may be a little "down" today.

IN TOUCH

Lord, my heart goes high and deep,
takes a dip and then a leap.
What a wonder that You keep
so in touch with all who weep
until we can dance and leap.

When we're feeling very small,
seem to shrink and barely crawl,
crushed against a cruel wall,
worry if we, too, should fall,
journey with us high or deep
so our sinking hearts can leap.

Take turns reading this with someone else, with each of you alternating. Make a speech choir and share it together.

How does the Lord allow you to dance and leap?

Write your own prayer asking God to continue to change your "low" days and make them into "high" days.

LOVE

Lord of disco, Lord of dance,
Lord of lovers' new romance,
see me as I take and live,
fall in love, receive, and give.
See me as I sacrifice,
feel the joy of wedding rice.
See me as I dance and dine
in some happy lover's line.
Lord of disco, Lord of dance,
come with love into romance.

Notice how music is related to love and affection. What do you think it's like to "fall in love?" Have you ever been in love? How does it feel?

Ask some grandparents or senior citizens how they fell in love. Listen and watch older couples sharing their love with each other.

Plan to spend some time talking with someone you like a lot. Be yourself; don't try to be someone you're not. Enjoy the relationship.

GOOD AND BAD DAYS

Lord of trumpets, God of praise,
turn my nights into Your days.
Give my spirit awe to gaze
at the wonder of Your days.
So unfold me in this maze
that my mouth will give You praise.
What a miracle of ways
cutting through your nights and days.

We all have good and bad days. When was your last bad day?

Recall what happened. What made it bad? What made your last good day good? Share these feelings with someone else.

Say a special prayer to the Lord today and say thanks for both good and bad days. Write the prayer and share it, or post it as a reminder.

DECISIONS

Lord,
I need to pick and choose,
must decide to win or lose,
pick things up that fall and break,
know when I should give or take.

Lord,
I need to say, "I will,"
till my heart is calm and still,
say once more, "I will," "I won't,"
then go out and do and don't.

Lord,
I need to pick and choose,
while they watch me win and lose.
You have walked inside these shoes,
where I daily win or lose.

Sometimes it's hard to make decisions. Think of the last three choices you had to make. Were they easy or hard? Did you do the "right" thing?

Think of some choices you will make next week. How do you go about making choices? What sort of system do you use to make decisions? Talk to your family about how they make choices.

It is especially good to know that even when we make the "wrong" choice our Lord is always there to forgive and forget. Thank the Lord for Divine presence and love for you today and ask for guidance in the decisions that need to be made.

44

RELATION-SHIP TO GOD

THE BASICS

Lord,
what I need You will provide.
Search to find me deep inside;
keep Your laws lest all collide;
help the molecules divide;
make all enemies allied;
open vistas yet untried.
Lord, Your mercy does provide
what will heal us deep inside.

Thank God today for providing you with the basics in which to live—food, shelter, security. Make up a special list of these gifts.

What are some "untried vistas" that you would like the Lord to open for you? Think of some possibilities in your future days ahead.

With God, everything is possible. Make a list of some "impossible hopes" and dreams you have that you'd like to see come true. And think about why you'd like these things to happen.

A ROCK INSIDE

Lord,
there's a rock inside my shoe,
hurts so bad, what shall I do?
So I'm going very slow,
for it is so hard to go.

When there's something in the shoe
what, O Lord, am I to do?
There's a limp inside my run,
how it cuts into my fun,
makes me even miss the sun.
There's a rock inside my shoe
in the walk I have with you.

What kind of "rocks" get into your shoes? Think of events, happenings, and people that cause you pain and grief.

Who helps you get those "rocks" out of your shoe (your life?) Thank them for their ministry to you.

Knowing and loving the Lord doesn't mean that everything goes well and harm will never happen. Knowing and loving the Lord means that we can accept those "rocks" in our shoes because we know the Lord is with us, guiding us and directing our every step.

MESSAGES

Lord of story; God of ode,
tap your Word through Morse code;
for each message choose the mode
that will keep us on the road,
lest we fall down with our load.
Lord of story, God of ode
make our going your abode.

What's your favorite story? Tell it to someone this week. Hear their story.

God comes to us in many ways. Recall some of your favorite stories in the Scriptures. What makes them important to you?

Write a story of your own life, up to the present. Notice how you have been a part of God's life.

PICK ME UP

Lord,
there's snow upon my feet;
the walking's slick on frozen sleet,
So pick me up if I fall down
and break my soul and break my crown.

Lord,
I'm walking on some eggs;
I'm shaking hard inside my legs.
So pick me up if I fall down
and break my soul and break my crown.

Lord,
I'm falling on my knees,
stumbling over stumps and trees.
So pick me up if I fall down
and break my soul and break my crown.

Lord,
I'm back again upon the road,
have a grip upon the load.
So pick me up if I fall down
and break my soul and break my crown,

Lord,
I'm walking right along;
thank You for the trees and song.
So pick me up if I fall down
and break my soul and break my crown.

We are all hard on ourselves once in awhile. Think of such times.

Why do you think you sometimes feel this way about yourself?

Try to remember some time you felt the way the prayer suggests: stumbling, shaking, breaking.

OPEN UP!

Lord, Your Son is at my door,
Jesus, whom the saints adore,
standing quiet at my door,
whether I am rich or poor.
Once You open up this door,
You keep coming more and more.

What if I were such a bore
that You'd stay outside my door?
Make my spirit Thee adore;
make me tender more and more
to those walking through my door.

This poem helps remind us that God has sent Jesus into our lives, who is always with us—to love, heal, comfort, share, forgive.

Think of times when you do not feel the Lord's presence. Why not?

Think of times when you are most likely to feel God's presence. What makes the difference? Rejoice in God's presence!

SHEEP AND SHEPHERD

Lord, the mountain cliffs are steep,
crevice edges long and deep.
Lord of children, Lord of sheep,
see how lambs in April leap?
Newborn lambs do run and leap
then go tumbling in the deep.
Make us sure that you will keep
careful watch for every sheep.
Lord of sheep and newborn lamb,
tell me who I am, I am.
Be my Shepherd when I weep,
be my holy paschal sheep
so my spirit too can leap,
over cliffs and through the deep.

We are sheep of the Good Shepherd, Jesus Christ. Shepherds watch their sheep so no harm comes to them. Think of ways that Christ the Good Shepherd, has guarded and protected you. Share one or two examples with someone.

Scripture compares us to sheep. How do you feel being compared to an animal? Is it a good comparison? Why?

Look through the Scriptures and see how the Bible uses *sheep* and *shepherds*. Use a concordance to study these two words.

SILENCE

Lord, the wheel of flour mill
stands so quiet, is so still.
All is silent, still, until
water turns the water mill.
There is deep inside of me
silent, waiting energy.
When I'm quiet as a mill,
comes the words of Christ, "I will."

You and I know that I will,
yes, I will, I will, I will.
When I'm quiet, when I'm still
spirit turns the water mill.

Have you ever seen a flour mill or a water mill? If not, ask around until someone can explain their reactions to them.

How can you be compared to such a mill? Think of as many ways as possible. Ask others to do the same.

Just like a mill, nothing happens until it is moved and turned by an outside force. This is just like the Christian life—the Spirit enables us to share and move and live in the name of Jesus.

See the "I will" of Jesus in the Garden of Gethsemane. How did Jesus struggle with "I will?" How do you?

THE KEY

Lord, I think I found the key
that unlocks that part of me
to reveal my melody.
There is deep inside of me
with the tiny melody
Spirit of the Trinity.
    Help me find the melody.
    Send the song of chickadee;
    let me hear some bumblebee,
    and some music rhapsody,
    till the song inside of me
    turns into Your melody.

This poem expresses hope of sharing pent-up feelings and joys of a young person. Think of a time when you had feelings that you found hard to express. What did you do to express them?

Think of a popular song that expresses how you feel today. Ask a friend to share a feeling in song with you.

Listen and reflect on some of the popular songs being played this week. What do they communicate to the listener? What is the general theme of many of them? Do they express some of your feelings? Is it always easy to release feelings of joy? What helps you do it? Who does it well?

GOD REVEALS

God is moving, God reveals
what the world sometimes conceals.
God is spirit, God reveals
what my heart and spirit feels.

The Lord is making things happen in your life. Where did you see the Lord at work in life today?

The Lord is active, but Satan is also very much alive in the world. How was Satan made visible to you today? What do you do about it? To whom can you tell what is evil to you?

What are some things that the world conceals from you? Or can you think of areas where the priorities of the world are different from the priorities of the people of God?

POWER

Lord,
You made the world so round,
water, fire fills the ground,
filled with silence, full of sound,
supersonic speed and sound;
and I know you're all around,
know the sights and all the sound
of this old creation ground.
Lord of heavens, God of ground,
spin Your supersonic ground
eons after we're around.

This prayer recalls the infinite might and majesty of God. God is worthy to be worshipped! Think of some of the wonders of God's world. Make a list of them and share them.

Read Genesis 1 and imagine the beginning of the world. Read further and marvel at God's work and power.

Make your own "Seven Wonders of the World" list. What do you consider to be God's greatest handiwork?

SINGING

Lord, the air is full of singing,
angel alleluias ringing
sounds of voice and nature bringing
celebration, new beginning
to this place of joyful singing.
Lord, the air is full of singing,
joy and love are ever winging
inside me and unto Thee.
Oh, what sounds there are to see,
for Your people, even me.

What are some of your top songs this week? Why do you like them?

What are the messages that come through the popular songs today? Are any of them dealing with faith, and hope, and joy? In what ways?

Try writing a song. Use a favorite tune and put your own words to it. Sing it to someone! And celebrate the gift of music!

Visit a person who writes poems and music or who directs a choir. Let them relate their feelings of music to you.

HOLY HUDDLE

Lord,
when temptations us befuddle
and we're caught inside a muddle
lead us to some holy huddle.

What are some of your temptations in life? Think about them for a little while and consider why they are such temptations.

Think of ways that you can deal with temptation. Are there ways of sharing them, confessing them, overcoming them?

The church, the people of God, is one place to go to overcome temptation. The Church is our holy huddle, where people can confess and be forgiven through Jesus Christ. Thank the Lord for some special people in your own "holy huddle" today.

PROMISES

Lord, You made the flood go down,
dried the mountain to the ground
in the roaring water sound.
So, I too, feel safe and found.

Lord, You made the valleys high;
lift me up when I must cry.
Raise me, too, when I will die.

In Your water and Your Word
You become the saving Lord.
Send Your promise and rainbow
so I know what still is so.

What is God's promise to each of us? What difference does that make in our daily lives?

What promises have you made to God or to other people lately? Are you following through on them? How do you feel about promises you make?

Have you broken any promise lately? Which one? How does that make you feel? Have others broken promises to you?

WINNERS

Lord of losers, God of cross,
join me in my win and loss.
Heal me when I turn and toss.
Seal me with Your empty cross.

Things do not always go right for us. Problems arise, we goof things up, people are hurt and disappointed. Think over the past week. What were some of your problems and failures that occurred? Share them.

God turns us losers into winners, through Jesus' death and resurrection. Tell people who are down this week that they are real winners because of Christ. Recall their reaction when they hear this.

Make a button out of cardboard or paper that says, "I'm a winner!" Wear it today and see how people react. Share with them that we all are winners in the Lord!

PONDER

Lord,
do You look up or upside down,
to scan the wholenss of my town?

Can You look up through fire and earth
to watch a seedling having birth?

Do You command an aerial view?
Can You look in while looking through?

Do You see seasons so unfold
that olden times are never old?

Can You keep looking from the top
so nothing ever seems to stop?

Do You see me from inside out
and know what soul is all about?

And are there other ways to see
that are still deep inside of me?

How do you imagine God? What does reading Psalm 139
do for you?

This prayer raises many questions about the Lord. Which ones have you also thought about? Ask others the same questions.

List other questions you have about the Lord. Ask them of someone.

How do you doodle? Through words or pictures or music or other activities? Make or say or write some "doodles" that picture how you see the Lord at work in the everyday-ness of your life.

SECRETS

Lord, I too have tried and tried
to open secrets deep inside.
    Lord, I too have tried and tried
    to see how love is deep and wide.
Sometimes when I prayed and sighed
faith inside was magnified.
    Send Your Spirit deep inside,
    wipe the tears that I have cried.
What was tiny now is wide;
what was dead is glorified.

Share what you think this poem is getting at with a friend of yours.

Think about some hidden secrets you have locked up in your mind. Why do you hide them? Will anyone ever know them? Would you feel better if somehow you could share them?

Write a poem that depicts some of the same feelings you receive from this prayer.

NATURE

SIGNS OF PRESENCE

Lord,
if I could dive into the sea
I know I'd find a sign of Thee.

If I could soar into a star
I'd find a part of where You are.

If I could climb some mountain side
You'd be so near I sure must hide.

If I could dig inside my mind
I know the One I'd surely find.

If I could search eternity
I know I'd meet Your Trinity.

If I could find the life in death
I'd feel the breathing of Your breath.

Lord, if I could fly on sparrow wing
I'd find You in the fluttering.

Look through the Psalms and choose some meanings that correspond to this prayer. The psalmist, too, saw the presence of God in all things.

Only through Christ are we able to affirm that God is in all things. His death and resurrection make it possible for us to see all things as gifts. Make a list of "If I could . . ." statements similar to this prayer.

Look and listen for signs and symbols of the presence of the Lord in TV and radio ads and magazine advertisements. Share them with others.

MORE QUESTIONS

Lord,
how do old and young reform?
Where is spring till it turns warm?

How do mountains become old?
Can a piece of sky be sold?
How do roses face the cold?

How do tides connect to moon?
Which is taller, night or noon?
Which is wiser, owl or loon?

Keep alive the heart and eye
when I ask You how and why.

Think of questions that are unanswerable. Isn't it good to know that there are no answers for some questions—or are there, and we just don't know them?

Make a list of questions you'd like answered. Then ask some folks and see what they respond.

God gives us minds to think and create. It's fun to ask and dig and question and study. Thank the Lord for these gifts today by using your talents to ask questions and search for answers.

TIMES AND SEASONS

Lord,
thank You for the times and seasons
storing all my hopes and reasons.
Thank You that I may remember
pumpkin pie in good November.
Thank You for the special seasons
forming very special reasons:
yellow roses in September,
Christmas tree in late December.
Lord, so form my times and reasons
into sometimes holy seasons.

What is your favorite time of year? Why? Take a survey with other members of your family.

What is your favorite holiday? Why? What are some favorite customs you have for this special time of year?

Every day is a Holy-day for the people of God, because Christ is present with us. Think of some special ways that you can celebrate next Monday and the first Wednesday of next month. Think of a way to celebrate an event or a person.

BLINKING LIGHTS

Lord,
the city lights keep on blinking,
good and bad seem to be winking.
And I sometimes have been thinking
if the meaning of this blinking
be your Holy Spirit winking.

Lord,
may there be a way of linking
all this red and yellow blinking

to the angel chorus winking?
Turn the city lights and blinking
into Holy Spirit winking
for my spirit and my thinking.

Think of the number of lights you have seen this week—
make a list of the many signs and symbols around you. What are
they communicating?

Jesus calls us the "lights of the world." How were you a
"light" to someone recently?

What kind of light do you most associate? Ask a group of
people to share the kind of light that symbolizes their faith.

DAYDREAMS

Lord, my mind has soared,
and I again am drawn toward
the mountain tops that You have poured,
to depths of jewels You have stored,
to rattles of the April gourd,
to vicious hurricanes that roared.

Lord, my simple heart has soared
through nature gifts and Holy Word
so You, oh Lord, may be adored.

Do you ever daydream? If so, about what? Is the Lord ever
in your daydreams?

Read over some of the Psalms that also marvel at God's
power and majesty. Make some comparisons between this
prayer and what the psalmist recorded.

When is the best time for you to think about the Lord?
Why is that? Talk with others and ask them to share these same
concerns. It should be some good conversation.

MUSIC

Lord,
I tingle and I shiver,
hearing how the cellos quiver,
how the foghorns pierce the river;
wind gust roaring through the trees,
sometimes whispers through the breeze.

So I behold a mystery
inside my own history
of trees and wind and autumn breeze
and in the nightboats of the river,
and in the music, light, and quiver.
In all this Lord, deliver
me
to Thee.

What sounds are you hearing right now? How can they remind you of the Lord? Make some connections.

Have you ever gotten "goosebumps" when you've heard a song or shared something special? Describe these special times to someone close to you.

What sounds remind you the most of God's love for you? Take a survey and see how other people respond also.

THE TREE AND THE SEA

Lord, I've chosen me a tree.
The tree was once on back of Thee.
And now I've chosen me a sea.
It is the sea of Galilee.
Your tree and sea are part of me.

God has given us creation as a gift. What are some of your special parts of creation?

Draw or sketch some of your favorite creations. Give it away as a gift.

Spend some time in your special space this week.

Thank the Lord for the sea of Galilee and the tree of Calvary today.

HUMMING BIRD

Lord,
I see the humming bird,
fastest humming I have heard,
and it seems so quite absurd
not to thank for what I heard.
Lord of life and humming bird,
keep me busy in Your Word.

Isn't it good that God made a humming bird? Have you watched one? They are so small and quick and amusing.

Take time today to look at other "small" things in your life. Be aware of all the great gifts from God—a barking dog, leaves of different shapes, colors, sounds, voices, old things, new things.

Write a prayer thanking God for the "little" things in life—even humming birds!

ETERNITY

Lord,
we plant a walnut tree
to hand on as heredity.
We know that we shall never see
the seed become a towering tree.
But some will come one day to Thee,
and bless Thee under walnut tree
for feelings old and feelings free
which point into eternity.
Lord,
in tiny things from Thee,
we peek into infinity.

What will people remember about you 100 years from now? What would you like them to remember?

Consider planting something that will continue to grow even after you have died. Some people plant trees and bushes to enjoy the growing process.

What could you do during your lifetime that would be remembered in years to come? Think of small things that become big and important things for people with whom they are shared.

WINTER

> Lord,
> all nature has a fresh snow cap,
> for catching winter in its lap,
> while all do sleep in trusting nap.
> I feel my spirit cheer and clap,
> for all the ways You warm and wrap
> Your nature in a winter cap.
> When all the sugar maple sap
> lies dormant in a season nap,
> asleep in mother nature's lap,
> refresh me, too, in winter wrap.

Recall how it feels to be out on a winter day, crunching in the sub-zero cold. Share your experience with someone. How does the cold affect you? If you never have had this experience, ask someone who has.

Think of ways that snow could be compared to God's love. Dream and imagine.

Sing a winter song to yourself or someone. Celebrate winter today, even if it isn't cold. Capture the mood of the season.

ANIMAL ARK

> Lord of forest, God of ark,
> countryside and city park,
> painted turtle, turning shark,
> soaring eagle, meadow lark,
> pigeon cooing, beagle bark,
> meet us in Your constant ark.

How is today's world like God's ark of the past? Do you see any connections?

Think of your favorite animals. Make a mental list of them and think through why you like these special species.

What can you do to help some animals who are becoming extinct in our world? What difference does it make?

EVERGREEN

> Lord of pointed evergreen,
> show me forces still unseen.
> When a time gets tough and mean,
> tell me of a life serene
> through Your Christmas evergreen.

How is your life like an evergreen? Are there some comparisons?

Christ's birth and death are also connected to an evergreen. The Christmas tree reminds us of His birth, and the wooden cross on Good Friday reminds us of His death. What do trees remind you of, in your life?

The evergreen tree is a symbol of God's constant presence in and with us. Trees point up and reach down. Thank God for trees today—and also for the cross and the evergreen.

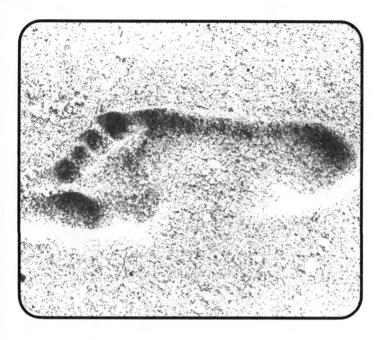

COAST TO COAST

Lord, Your word is coast to coast.
Lift our bread, You are the host.
Lift the butter, lift the toast.
Lift potatoes, lift the roast.
You are Lord, and You are host,
sea to sea and coast to coast.

How does this prayer compare to Psalm 150? Read and share both of them together.

Look at everyday things today and try to see the Lord in them. Look at little things in different ways today. The Lord is there!

Do you know people from "coast to coast?" If so, send or phone them this prayer as a reminder of your friendship with them.

SMELLS

Lord,
where do You store the fragrant smell
of blossoms that I know so well?
By some aromas I can tell
when all is calm and all is well.
How much there is for me to tell
when I recall a hidden smell.
All earth is like an altar smell.

Think of some smells that are favorites of yours. Why did you choose them?

Think of smells that you dislike. Do you know of people who like those smells?

What does your altar at church "smell" like? Why? What does this smell remind you of? How should an altar smell?

TREASURES

Lord,
I cannot ever measure
all the value of Your treasure.
It is so high;
it is so wide
as desert sky
and mountainside.
Lord, I cannot ever measure
all the value of the pleasure
You made for me:

the morning sky,
the midnight sea.

I wonder why
I do not always measure
this marvel of Your treasure.

There is so much about life that we cannot ever begin to understand. God's power and majesty is something to behold. What are some of the exciting incomprehensible ideas about God?

Take some time today to marvel at God's creation. Take time to look at the little things around you. Thank God for them. Make a list of the "little treasures" you have all around you that are so often taken for granted.

List some of your favorite events in creation. Why are they your favorites? Share your list with other friends, and ask them to share.

SUMMER SCENES

Lord, the earth is royal green.
Show my spirit sights unseen.
Should I lose what is serene,
send my eyes an evergreen.

What time of year do you like best? Why?

How do you feel about this time of year? What do you like or dislike about it?

What season of the year do you feel like today— winter, summer, spring, or fall? Why? Ask others to share with you their feelings about the seasons. See how they react to this poem.

How does God continue to give us an "evergreen?"

RESUR-
RECTION/
SACRAMENT

SUFFERING SERVANT

Lord,
it's sad enough to make me sob
the way they hurt You on the job.
They turned into a raging mob.
They came to take You and to rob
You in the middle of Your job—
working down beside the stone,
praying hard, and not alone.

Recall for a moment the suffering and death that our Lord went through for all of us. Say a prayer of thanksgiving and joy.

Think of ways that the world is still causing suffering. Confess how today you were part of that suffering.

Rejoice in God's forgiveness of you through Christ's suffering and death. Share a prayer of thankfulness for Christ's resurrection that frees us from suffering and death.

SPECIAL EYES

Lord, You give us special eyes;
show us where to find Your prize.
Lead us by Your new surprise,
into what we may surmise.

Lord, You give us special eyes;
help us search Your starry skies,
sort through faith and see the lies
which can dim our wishful eyes.
Help us to be hopeful, wise,
seeing where the future lies.

Where is the best place to find the Lord? Ask a number of people that question this week and make a list of the responses.

Where do you find the Lord most often? Start with Christ's death and resurrection and see where it leads you. Chances are, you'll have a whole new perspective on life if this is where you begin.

God comes to us in many ways, especially through Word and sacraments. Thank the Lord for your pastors and educators and parents who have taught you and who continue to share this faith with you.

RESURRECTION

Lord of mountains, God of hay,
when we once in silence lay
nothing more to do or say
take us swift where angels pray
and where angels dance and sway
on the everlasting way.
Lord of eons, God of day,
greet us with Your grand "Hooray!"

This is a prayer about death. Send it to someone who has just experienced death. Add your own thoughts to it.

We can meet death with a grand "Hooray!" because Christ has been resurrected from the grave. That is our hope, that is our joy! Think of this often as you hear what the world says about death and how often people try not to talk about it. Christ has conquered death for us!

Write out a brief summary of what you would like to have someone say at your funeral. How do you want people to remember you? Share it with someone. And save it for future use!

AMAZING

Lord,
how good that we can be amazed,
that You once crucified are now so praised.
In the midst of glory we are dazed.
So quickly clear our sight when eyes are glazed;
Lord, each day or night we wish to be amazed.

Think once again of the Resurrection account of Christ. Read it to yourself in Mark 16. See it.

Sometimes we act as though Christ did not rise from the grave. We allow "stones" to get in our way of seeing that the tomb is empty. What are some of these "stones" in your life that prevent you from seeing that the stone has been rolled away?

Create a resurrection cheer. Shout it out—to yourself, to friends, to your whole world!

EUCHARIST

Lord,
the bread is broken,
the words of institution spoken.
This little bread is more than token.
Your blood is shed, Your body broken.

Lord,
the wine is blessed and poured,
imagination now has soared.
Your life and spirit is outpoured.
All life to come now be adored,
for love and energy outpoured.

The Lord's Supper refreshes and renews us. Plan to celebrate the Sacrament the very next chance you get.

God comes to us in small ways—through bread and wine and water. Be thankful for the little things in your life also. They, too, become big and important to us.

Use this prayer the next time you celebrate the Lord's Supper. And share it with your pastor, who may put it in the bulletin. Or write your own and give it to the church as a gift.

CONCEAL AND REVEAL

Lord,
You know the way I feel,
how I sometimes wheel and deal,
lose my interest and my zeal,
strike a bargain and a deal,
turn a friend into a heel,
fail to thank You for a meal,
underrate Your love appeal.
Spirit, enter in my zeal.
God, I ask that You reveal
what I sometimes would conceal.

We sin daily. We fail our Lord, ourselves, and others. Confess to God the sins that you recall from today. Ask for forgiveness. And know that God does forgive you, through Christ's death and resurrection.

Make a list of your "pet" problems. Share them with a good friend, or at least with the Lord. After confessing them, rip them up and throw them away, reassured that Christ has forgiven them.

Go to someone who you have recently harmed or hurt in some way and ask their forgiveness. Share this joy of forgiveness with them.

FOOD AND DRINK

Lord of vineyard, God of wine,
teach me how to drink and dine
in this daily life of mine.
Life is Yours and life is mine;
You are human and divine.
Get me past each tiny line.

Lord of angels, God of mine,
lead us in the food and wine
into worlds of love divine.

God gives us good things to eat and to drink. Recall
everything you ate and drank today. Quite a variety is available.

The Lord comes to us in many ways. In small things, like
bread and wine and water, God gives us the Holy Meal and the
washing of Baptism. Thank the Lord for the little things in life
today.

How has the Lord shared His love with you today?

BAPTISM

Lord of water, God of love,
send Your spirit and Your dove
from inside and from above,
so my sleepy heart may move
in the energy of love.

Lord, You made Your Son so brave,
brave enough to seek and save,
not to fear the roaring wave,
not to worry in the grave.
So make us both sure and brave
when we face both life and grave.

Read again the account of the baptism of Jesus in Mat-
hew 3.

Ask someone what their baptism means to them. Share
what your baptism means to you, too.

What does your baptism have to do with your death? Ask
someone to discuss it with you.

THE SACRAMENT

Lord,
when my spirit cannot tell
what is sick and what is well—
when my spirit does not know
what is wrong and what is so—
when my spirit will not run
in Your play and in Your fun,
make my spirit confident
in your Holy Sacrament.

The Holy Sacrament, the Lord's Supper, gives us strength to deal with concerns and problems of our lives. Plan to celebrate the Sacrament as soon as possible.

Share this thought with someone who is not feeling well today. Read it, send it, share it with this person. And tell him or her what it means to you.

Remember this prayer the next time you feel down and out. It may help you remember the power of the Lord's presence in your life.

FOOD

Lord, see my overflowing plate,
the food I drank, the food I ate.
See all those who come too late,
find no food upon their plate,
those who weep while they still wait.
Can I trust if I must wait?
Would my waiting turn to hate?
Lord, bless this food upon my plate.

Why is it that many people are starving for food while we have so much? What are some things you can do to help people be more aware of the hunger in this world? Make a list of possible responses. Here are some for a start:

> Consider what you eat. Are there ways to cut out some of the junk food or to eat less?

> Find books on hunger in the library. Read about the food conditions in the world.

> Ask your church to sponsor hunger days and emphasize hunger. Volunteer your services.

> Consider a vocation that would help to share more of the gifts of God to others.

MEALTIME

> Lord of pear and apple cake,
> morning dew and summer lake,
> meet us in the bread we make.

Lord of soup and navy bean,
casserole and worlds unseen,
meet us if the times be lean.

> Lord of cafes, menu rhyme,
> growing season, standard time,
> meet us in our suppertime.

Lord of pizza pies to take,
baggie lunch and layered cake,
meet us in the meal You make.

> Lord of life and summer wheat,
> sweet potato, sugar beet,
> bless the drink and bread we eat.

Write down five to seven of your favorite things in life. Make a short prayer about them.

Use this prayer at mealtimes with family and friends.

How many of the items mentioned do you like? Which ones could you do without? Are they gifts of God even if you don't care for them? Thank God for the things you like and also for the things others like.

CHANGES

GROWTH

How is it, Lord, You made me grow?
I feel the change from head to toe.
  What some don't see, I know is so.
My mood is high and often low,
  for good and bad come in a row.
I sometimes feel I finally know
  some special things You know are so.

So in these things that frustrate me,
  help me for sure once more to see
that life is new, and I am free
  after the hurt comes out of me.

O what an honor it must be
to handle all eternity.

Think of ways that you have grown in the past year. What changes happened to you physically? How do you feel about these changes? Who do you talk to about feelings?

Look into the mirror. What do you see? Are you proud of what you see? Did you know that God made only one of each of us! That must make you and me important.

Take time to write out or think of a special prayer of thanks to the Lord who loves you and keeps you growing and in the faith.

NEW BIRTH

Lord,
reinforce the tiny tree
growing strong inside of me.
    Give my tree a simple name.
Things will never be the same
if that tree will finally be
tree of God inside of me.
I must tell You when I see
all this life inside of me,
green and new as life can be.
    This is my nativity.

What is meant by "the tiny tree" inside of you? Describe it to someone. Ask them to tell you what they see.

Christ's birth gives us the joy that Christ lives in us each and every day. God's spirit makes us stronger in this faith. Write a brief "creed" that shares what you believe in, on the basis of Christ's birth, death, and resurrection.

"New birth" happens each day for us as God continues to grow in us through faith. Share your faith with someone special today.

FUTURE

Lord,
see the future I must face,
the big, wide world I must embrace.
I feel I'm running in their race
in losing time and final place.
Is this the place I am to be?
Is this my best reality?

Lord,
I need a lot of love and grace
if I am truly going to face
this world You want me to embrace.
Your love and time in human race
shows me the life I can embrace.
Give me such love that I might face
with confidence what I embrace.

Project what you may be doing five or ten years from now.
Are you excited or afraid of the future? Explain your feelings to
someone.

List what you would like to see happen in the world within
the next five years. Do this with your family or with other friends.

If you could change two or three things in your life within
the next one or two years, what would you change? Express your
feelings to someone else.

MY BODY

Lord,
   my nose is getting very long;
my changing voice breaks in the song.
   Some hair is coming on my face;
my feet are taking too much space.
   They say this changing is my age.
"Hang on," they say. "It's just a stage."
   You see the blemish on my nose?
How differently the body grows?
   How others step upon my toes?
Lord,
   this growing who I am to be,
can be Your gift inside of me.

Look in the mirror and notice some changes in your face and body. What do you like about what you see? What would you like to change?

God has given us our bodies. They are gifts. They change and grow. One way to thank the Lord for your body is to take care of it through rest, food, and exercise. Evaluate how you are treating your body and how you can improve on its treatment.

Look in that mirror again—and repeat to yourself—"I am me, and I am glad." Accept yourself. You are God's gift to others.

BIRTH AND DEATH

Lord of death and sudden birth,
give us life inside the earth.
Turn us soon from tears to mirth.
Oh, the wonder and the worth
we do have in second birth.

Lord of ashes, joy and tear,
laughter, crying, sudden fear,
stand beside our funeral bier,
showing us how God is near.
When both joy and fear appear
make us sure that God is near.

What would you share with someone who has just experienced the loss of a loved one through death? Think about it for awhile. Ask your pastor or another friend what they say to people who are grieving.

What is it that Christians can rejoice in, even in the midst of death? Share the Good News with someone today!

Read the obituary columns in your newspaper. Say a prayer for grieving loved ones or write about these people who have died. Share it with someone.

AGING

Lord,
keep my soul from being old
and my heart from growing cold.
Keep my love from being sold.

Lord,
I wish one day if I be old
to come as child, and still behold

how hope is warm when death is cold,
how love is free when all is sold.

Think a moment how you will feel when you are 75 years old. What would you like to be doing at that age? How do you think you'll be feeling and acting?

Ask some older persons how they feel about their age. Are they happy? Sad? Depressed? Living in the past? Hoping for the future? Share a little more of yourself with them.

Make a commitment to yourself to rejoice each day in new life and to see old age not as a disease, but as a gift from God. And why not go visit some older folks and share this with them also!

TRAFFIC

Lord, the people come and go.
It makes the going very slow,
all this steady traffice flow
in this traffic jam below.
    Lord of traffic, God of flow,
    when we line up in a row,
    when the going seems so slow,
    keep Your spirit in the flow
    in this constant stop and go.

Traffic jams can be frustrating. Have you ever experienced getting caught in traffic when you were trying to get somewhere? What did you do about it?

How would you solve traffic jams? Think of some possible solutions. Ask others what they would do.

What are some positive things one could do when stuck in a traffic jam? Invent creative ways to respond to jam-ups, and use them the next time you're caught in a jam.

DIRECTIONS

Lord, You made the East and West,
river gorges, mountain crest;
all directions You did make.
How am I to choose to take
North or South or East or West?
Which direction is the best?
Inside all diversity
give my heart more clarity.

Which part of the country do you like best—North, South, East or West? Why?

In which part of the country or world would you like to live? Why?

Discuss why you think the Lord made so many different kinds of scenery and geography. Wouldn't it have been easier for us if He would have made the land the same all over? Share the good things about variety of landscapes, cultures, and societies.

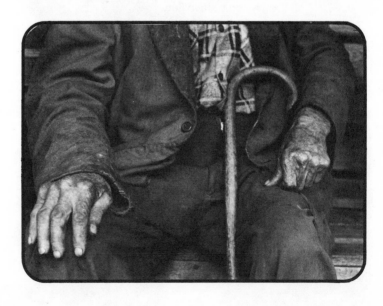

ENERGY INSIDE

>Lord,
>help me face anxiety,
>inside insecurity.
>Feed my soul in energy
>of the Holy Trinity.

What scares you about sexuality? Try to identify some of your concerns and fears. Talk to a friend about them.

Who is it in your life that you can talk to about anything that is troubling you? Identify one person you could talk with about any subject. If you cannot think of someone, why not try to identify a person this week to talk to.

Pray to the Lord today for the presence and power to overcome your anxieties and fears.

STILL MORE QUESTIONS

>Lord,
>we're lined up in a row,
>held in line by what is so.
>So afraid to bend and grow,
>holding tight to what we know.
>>What will happen when I know
>>all the things You know are so?
>>What will happen when I see
>>all the changing inside me?

Will there ever be a time when we know all there is to know? If so, when?

What prevents you from growing? What can you do about it?

What one question would you like to ask the Lord? Why?

SLOW ME DOWN

Lord,
my body's changing very fast.
What once was new will never last.
This day to come will soon be past.
What is to go, and what will last?
Lord, so much is going past,
so slow me down, when life is fast.

How much leisure time do you have—time to do what you want to do? How can you make more time yours, especially if you feel your life is going too fast?

Changes in the body can be scary, but also exciting. Exciting if you know what's happening—scary if you're not sure what is going on. Is your development and phsyical growth a blessing to you, or a problem? You might want to check out how others feel about their own growth also.

Think a moment, by yourself, what the Lord meant when He said, "Be still, and know that I am God . . ." Plan to get away by yourself soon. Reflect on God's presence in your world.

UNCHANGING

Lord of youth, God of old,
    what comes free and what is sold?
when will timid become bold?
    What will fall if I not hold?
What will crumple, finally fold,
    if we not be strong and bold?
When will iron turn to gold?
    When will summer become cold?
All Your laws are strong and old.
    Make us new and make us bold
While Your old creations hold.

God's laws remain true for us. Think of some "absolutes" that you connect with the Lord. Discuss them with a friend.

Many things continue to change, but God's love remains constant. List as many changes as you can that happened during the last year—in politics, sports, travel, economy, weather, neighbors, jobs, religion.

Share a prayer with your family or friend that tells of God's unchanging love for us. Share it often.

STOP AND GO

Lord,
behavior seems to stop and go.
What I knew I do not know.
So many words are stored in realms below,
where secret thoughts are dim and slow.
I need long seasons when I grow,
for life unfolds so fast and slow.
Lord, make my sky with Your rainbow
spanning every yes and no.

Think of barriers that have gotten in your way of getting something accomplished. What did you do about these?

How does God fit into some of your thoughts concerning what is right and wrong? How do you know what the Lord wants you to do?

What are three things that you would like to have happen to you within the next week? What if they did? Make a list of them and see what happens.

TIME

Lord, times keep flying by,
making day and evening sky.
Moon comes up, I wonder why;
autumn comes, the birds do fly.
Newborn babies come and cry.
Lord,
the times keep flying by.
Keep me saying, "Wow" and "Why?"

Think back over the past year. What significant changes have happened to you? Reflect on them.

Try this for the next week: as you get up each morning, say a little prayer to the Lord for a new day. It's a gift to you. You might even want to make this a habit.

Write or tell about some of the gifts the Lord puts into your life each day.